Anne's
glory box

Gloria McKinnon

Distributed By
Quilters' Resource Inc.
Chicago, IL 60614
1-312 278-5695

Contents

Introduction 3

Victorian Heart Frame 4

Silk Collage Memory Vest 10

Posies and Pansies 12

The Sisters 14

Violet Time 17

Victorian Sewing Box 20

Petit Point Brooch 24

Matrioshki Doll 26

Continental Pillow Covers 30

Autumn Glow 32

Roses and Lilacs Tea Cosy 34

Drunkard's Path Quilt 37

Lace Flower Basket 40

Smocked Dress 43

Strawberries 46

Editorial
Managing Editor: Judy Poulos
Editorial Assistant: Ella Martin
Editorial Coordinator: Margaret Kelly

Photography
Andrew Elton

Styling
Kathy Tripp

Illustrations
Lesley Griffith

Design and Production
Manager: Anna Maguire
Design: Jenny Pace
Layout: Lulu Dougherty
Picture Editor: Cheryl Dubyk-Yates

Published by J.B. Fairfax Press Pty Limited
80-82 McLachlan Ave
Rushcutters Bay, NSW 2011, Australia
A.C.N. 003 738 430
Formatted by J.B. Fairfax Press Pty Limited
Printed by Toppan Printing Company, Singapore

JBFP 422

ANNE'S GLORY BOX
Series ISBN 1 86343 166 7
Book 10 ISBN 1 86343 253 1

Hands Across the Sea

Through many years of travelling, attending shows and teaching overseas, I have made many 'Friends of the Store' and many 'Friends to Gloria'.

Through the pages of our books, you have already met many of my dear friends from America and New Zealand. In this book, we will introduce you to more of our overseas friends, including a brand-new friend from England.

Through these pages, we hope that you can enjoy and share the talents of these wonderful needlewomen and tutors. You can make your own unique versions of their work – all without leaving home!

Frequently, we are able to bring these special tutors to Australia to teach at Anne's Glory Box and those who have been lucky enough to attend theses classes, retain wonderful memories of their experiences. However, for those who are not able to be with us in person – this book is for you.

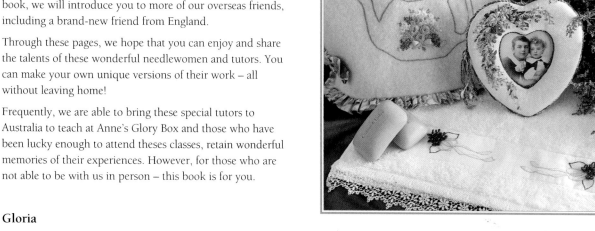

Gloria

Victorian Heart Frame

DESIGNED AND STITCHED BY JUDITH BAKER MONTANO, COLORADO

Frame those special memories in a beautiful heart-shaped frame, festooned with a spray of silk ribbon flowers. This nostalgic picture frame is a wonderful introduction to the art of silk ribbon embroidery.

Note: This frame and three other kits produced by Quilters' Resource in the United States are available from Anne's Glory Box.

Materials

- ❧ 23 cm x 92 cm (9 in x 36 in) of cream moiré fabric
- ❧ 18 cm x 54 cm (7 in x 21 in) of fleece
- ❧ 20 cm (8 in) of each of three 1 cm (³/₈ in) wide satin ribbons
- ❧ 76 cm (30 in) of each of two fancy cords
- ❧ 16.5 cm (6¹/₂ in) art board picture frame with a prop
- ❧ 76 cm (30 in) each of fourteen 4 mm (³/₁₆ in) wide silk ribbons
- ❧ 61 cm (24 in) of silk buttonhole twist thread
- ❧ beads, including small pearl beads
- ❧ 1 m (1¹/₈ yd) of Nymo thread
- ❧ Perle cotton
- ❧ beading needles
- ❧ chenille needle, size 22
- ❧ sharps needle, size 10
- ❧ water-soluble marker pen
- ❧ tracing paper
- ❧ pencil
- ❧ 15 cm (6 in) embroidery hoop
- ❧ spray adhesive
- ❧ craft glue
- ❧ scalpel or knife

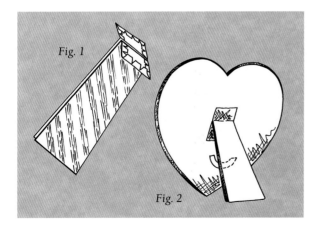

Fig. 1

Fig. 2

Method

See the Patterns and the Embroidery Design on the Pull Out Pattern Sheet.

1 Trace the floral design and the heart pattern onto the moiré, using the marker pen. Do not cut out the fabric yet. Secure the fabric into the hoop with the traced pattern facing upwards.

2 Make the concertina flowers first and sew them into place with the Nymo thread.

3 Following the ribbon embroidery guide on pages 7-9, work the remaining flowers. Use the buttonhole twist thread for the feather stitch. Highlight the embroidery with beads and small pearls.

Assembling

1 Remove the embroidery from the hoop. Mark 12 mm (¹/₂ in) beyond the solid pattern line on both the outer and inner edges. These are your cutting lines. Cut out the embroidered frame front. Erase any visible marks from the back with a wet cloth and cold water. Set the piece aside.

2 On the moiré fabric, mark two frame backs (without the inner heart opening) and two props. Cut them out 12 mm (¹/₂ in) beyond the solid pattern lines.

3 On the fleece, mark two frame fronts (with the heart opening) on the solid line and one 12 mm (¹/₂ in) beyond the solid line. Cut the hearts out on the marked lines.

4 Glue the three fleece hearts to the frame front, placing the larger fleece heart on top. This ensures a smooth edge when you fold the fleece to the back. Spray the top fleece with the adhesive and glue the finished embroidered front to the padded heart front. Clip along the inside and outside edges, stopping the scissors at the board's edge.

5 Fold the fabric edges around to the back and glue them in place.

6 For the frame back, spray one side of a board back with adhesive. Lay the wrong side of the moiré backing onto the sprayed area. Clip the moiré edges, then fold the fabric around to the back and stick it down.

7 Repeat step 3 to make another back. Glue the two backs firmly together, with the wrong sides facing, then weight them with books until the glue is dry.

8 Score each prop on the dotted line with the back of a knife or scalpel. Cover the unscored sides with moiré fabric as for the backs. Glue them together, leaving 2.5 cm (1 in) ends above the scoring free of glue (Fig. 1). Press the prop under books until the glue is dry.

9 Glue the front and back of the frame together along the bottom and sides, leaving the top portion free to insert a picture.

10 Decide on the angle of tilt of the frame, then glue the prop to the back at the appropriate angle. To ensure the prop stays put, measure the distance between the prop and the heart back, then cut this length from the remaining satin ribbon. Glue the ribbon from the prop to the back of the frame (Fig. 2).

11 Apply glue lightly along the frame's joined edges, then cover the edges with the twisted cords. Tie them in a knot on the side and let them hang in a tassel form.

Judith Baker Montano's Tips
for Silk Ribbon Embroidery

Template plastic
Use template plastic to make a window template for all the patterns.

Threading the ribbon
Remember, silk ribbon is delicate and will fray on the edges. Use a short length 30-40 cm (12-16 in).

Needle eye lock
Thread the ribbon through the eye of the needle. Pierce one end of the ribbon, directly in the centre and 6 mm (1/4 in) from the end with the point of the needle. Pull the long end of the ribbon and lock it into the eye of the needle.

Soft knot
Make the needle eye lock, then grasp the end of the ribbon and form a circle with the end of the ribbon and the point of the needle (A). Pierce the end of the ribbon with a short running stitch (B). Pull the needle and ribbon through the running stitch to form a soft knot.

Ribbon manipulation
Learn to use the ribbon properly. If it is pulled too tight or it twists too much, it will just look like a heavy thread. Use your free thumb to hold the ribbon flat against the fabric. Most stitches depend on the ribbon being flat. Keep the thumb in place while you stitch and tighten the ribbon over the thumb. This will remove any twists. A large needle or a knitting stitch holder can be used instead of your thumb.

Adjusting the ribbon
Sometimes the ribbon will fold up on itself as it passes through the fabric, and it has to be adjusted so the full width of the ribbon shows. Hold the ribbon flat under your free thumb and slide the needle under the ribbon, then gently slide the needle back and forth, from the thumb to the needle hole in the fabric.

Correct needles
Above all, use a chenille needle. Remember the heavier the fabric, the larger the eye of the needle you should use.

Silk Ribbon Embroidery Guide

Bullion-tipped lazy daisy stitch

A most effective variation of the simple lazy daisy stitch – a bullion stitch replaces the anchor stitch. The petal or leaf is changed, depending on the length of the lazy daisy stitch and the bullion stitch. Keep the ribbon flat and taut. Come up from the bottom at **A** and make a loop. Go down again at **A**. Come up at **B** (like a basic lazy daisy). Grasp the ribbon in your free hand and loop it under the point of the needle. Keep the ribbon flat. Wrap the ribbon around the needle two or three times. Hold the bullion twists in place with your thumb and pull the needle through. Hold the bullion knot firmly on the fabric and in line with the twists. Anchor the bullion knot by going down through the fabric again.

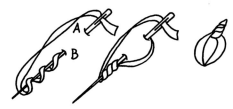

Colonial knot

A lovely little knot that sits up and has a little dimple in the centre – come up from the bottom at **A**. Form a backwards **C** with the ribbon. Insert the needle under the ribbon at the top of the backwards **C**. Now, grasp the ribbon and form a loop over and under the needle. This forms a figure 8 (**B**). Hold the needle vertically and pull the knot firmly around the needle. Insert the needle as close to the original hole (but not into it) as possible (**C**). Always hold the ribbon in place until the needle is pulled to the back. This forms a neat colonial knot.

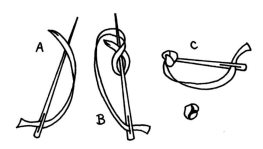

Concertina rose

Thread the needle, using thread that matches the ribbon, and knot the end. Use a 20 cm (8 in) length of ribbon. Fold the ribbon at a right angle in the centre (**A**). Fold the horizontal section of ribbon over and to the left (**B**). Bring the ribbon up on the bottom and fold it up and over (**C**). The folds will take on a square look (**D**). Keep folding from right side to top to left side to bottom until the ribbon is used up. Grasp the two ends in one hand and let go of the folded ribbon. It will spring up in accordion folds. Hold the two ends in one hand and pull gently down on one ribbon (it doesn't matter which one) until a rose is formed. With the knotted thread, go down through the top and up again. Do this two or three times. Finish on the bottom and wrap the base tightly, make a slip knot, and cut the thread, leaving a 15.5 cm (6 in) tail to sew down later. Cut the two ends of the ribbon as close to the base as possible.

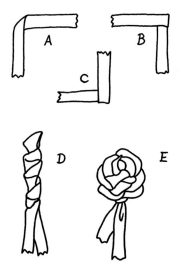

Curved whip stitch

Keep the ribbon flat. Make a straight stitch the desired length, **A** to **B**. Bring the needle up again at **A**. Wrap the straight stitch two or three times, working toward **B** and keeping the ribbon flat. Repeat the wraps working toward **A**. Anchor the last wrap stitch by passing the needle to the back. Crowd the stitch so it will curve.

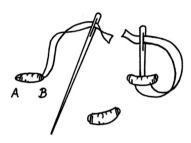

Feather stitch

This is a vertical stitch and alternates from right to left. It is worked from top to bottom. Begin with a single stitch. Come up at **A** and go down at **B**. Come up in the centre, below **A** and **B** at **C**. The secret is to always put the needle in at **B** straight across from where the thread came out at **A**.

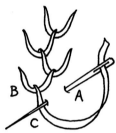

French knot

Bring the needle up and circle the ribbon twice around the needle. Hold the ribbon off to one side as you insert the needle in the fabric, as close to the starting point as possible. Hold the knot in place until the needle is pulled through.

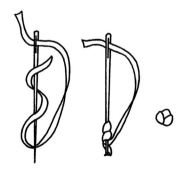

Japanese ribbon stitch

Come up under the fabric at point **A**. Make sure the ribbon lies flat by running the needle under the ribbon. Lay the ribbon flat on the fabric and pierce the ribbon in the centre at point **B**. Gently pull the needle through to the back. The ribbon will curl at the tip, but the whole effect will be lost if the ribbon is pulled too tightly. Petals and leaves can be varied by length, and by adjusting the tension of the ribbon before piercing, it can be quite loose.

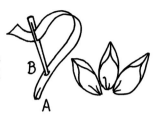

Lazy daisy stitch

This stitch is a free-floating chain stitch. Bring the needle up from the back and hold the ribbon flat with your thumb (**A**). Insert the needle at the starting point so the ribbon forms a loop. Bring the needle out a short distance away. The needle passes over the ribbon. Take a small anchor stitch at the top of the loop. Length of the stitch and the anchor can be varied.

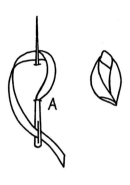

Montano knot

Designed for the effect and not for the technique! This glorified French knot is loose and effective for filling in and for floral sprays. Depending on the size desired, it varies from one to six twists. Bring the needle up from the back and circle the ribbon around the needle one to six times. Hold the ribbon very loosely and do not hold the ribbon off to one side. Insert the needle into the fabric as close to the starting point as possible. Do not pull tight; let the knot remain loose and flowery.

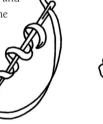

Plume stitch

Worked from top to bottom. Come up at **A** and go down 3 mm (1/8 in) away at **B**. Keep the ribbon flat at all times. Make a loop and control it with a round toothpick. Hold the loop in place with your thumb and come up at **C** piercing the fabric and ribbon. Form another loop. Continue down until the plume is finished.

Spider web rose

With Perle Cotton, form an anchor stitch. Come up at **A**, go down at **B** and bring the needle up in the centre of **A** and **B**, forming a V. With the needle over the thread, go down at **C**. Add a bar of the same length on each side forming five spokes. With the ribbon, come up in the centre of the anchor spokes and begin weaving over and under the spokes. Allow the ribbon to twist and keep it loose. Fill in until the spokes are covered.

Straight stitch

This stitch may be taut or loose depending on the flower petal. Come up from under the fabric at **A**. Take a stitch of the desired length and go down at **B**. Make sure the ribbon lies flat. Use your thumb to hold it flat or hold the ribbon in your free hand and run the needle under the ribbon to its point **A**.

Note: For a running stitch, continue in a straight line, keeping the ribbon flat.

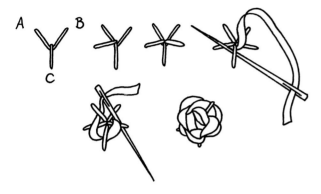

Silk Collage Memory Vest

Designed and stitched by Pat Flynn Kyser, Alabama

This elegant vest features special photographs that have meaning to you, or to the intended recipient of your vest.

Materials

- ❧ **photographs**
- ❧ **commercial vest pattern without darts**
- ❧ **sufficient homespun to cut two vest fronts**
- ❧ **sufficient solid-coloured taffeta to cut one vest back**
- ❧ **sufficient printed cotton fabric for lining**
- ❧ **freezer paper (the type sold in craft and patchwork shops)**
- ❧ **silk scraps or old neckties**
- ❧ **variety of hand- and/or machine-embroidery threads**
- ❧ **silk ribbon in a variety of colours and widths**
- ❧ **special tiny buttons, metal charms, scraps of lace, beads**
- ❧ **1.22 m (1^1/$_3$ yd) of 2 cm (^{3}/$_4$ in) wide grosgrain ribbon**
- ❧ **2.44 m (2^2/$_3$ yd) of 6 mm (^{1}/$_4$ in) wide grosgrain ribbon**
- ❧ **matching sewing threads**

Method

1 Cut out the front and back pieces from the homespun to use as a base. Set them aside for later use.

2 To transfer the photographs, cut a piece of homespun 21.5 cm x 28 cm (8^1/$_2$ in x 11 in) and a piece of freezer paper the same size. Iron the homespun to the waxed side of the freezer paper, then run this stiffened piece of fabric through a photocopier, copying the photos you have chosen onto it. Wait until the copy medium has had time to dry thoroughly, then cover the photos on the fabric with a pressing cloth and press to heat-set them. Cut them apart to use on your vest.

3 Using the pressed quilt method (described in steps 4 and 5) cover the vest fronts in oddly shaped scraps of silk. (If you use old ties, it is a good idea to take them apart and handwash the fabric, before using it.) Place the fabric photos into your collage, wherever they seem appropriate to the design. Work with both vest fronts, side by side, so that you make one side to complement the other, but do not mirror-image them.

4 Pin one silk scrap in place on one of the homespun vest fronts, right side up, then build around it with the other scraps, placing each new scrap right side down, sewing the joining seam, then flipping the new one right side up and pressing it in place. You can do this by hand or by machine.

5 When both vest fronts are covered, decorate all the seams with fancy stitching, either by hand or by machine. You can do a simple machine feather stitch, as Pat did, using a variety of silky-textured threads, or you can create an even more elaborate effect with hand-sewn decorative stitches and decorative threads.

6 Decorate around the photographs and other areas of the vest fronts with silk ribbon embroidery. Create nosegays and bouquets of flowers, adding additional embellishment in the form of bits of lace, tiny buttons, metal charms and beading.

7 Cut out the back of the vest. Break up the plain surface of the vest back by decorating it with several rows of machine-stitched grosgrain ribbon.

8 Cut out the vest linings. Follow the pattern instructions for the lining and for finishing the vest.

Finishing

Select a central section of the back of the vest and create the illusion of crazy pieces by feather-stitching random shapes in a thread to match the taffeta. Stitch through both the taffeta and the lining, letting the feather stitches 'quilt' the vest. Wear and enjoy your beautiful memory vest, or give it away, as Pat did – to a special daughter-in-law!

Posies and Pansies

MADE BY PIECEMAKERS COUNTRY STORE, CALIFORNIA

This beautiful appliqué block looks wonderful framed, made into a pillow or as the beginning of a fabulous appliqué quilt.

Finished block size: 35.5 cm (14 in) square

Materials

- ❧ 46 cm (18 in) of fabric for the background
- ❧ 11.5 cm (4½ in) of fabric for each pansy, or scraps of three fabrics
- ❧ 11.5 cm (4½ in) of fabric for flowers E and F
- ❧ scrap of fabric for the centre of F
- ❧ 11.5 cm (4½ in) of fabric for flowers G and H
- ❧ 11.5 cm (4½ in) each of three fabrics for the leaves
- ❧ embroidery floss for the stems
- ❧ fourteen buttons in a variety of sizes and colours
- ❧ 46 cm (18 in) each of wadding and fabric for the backing
- ❧ tracing paper
- ❧ black permanent fineline marker pen
- ❧ masking tape
- ❧ pencil
- ❧ cardboard or plastic for the templates

Method

See the Patterns and Placement Diagrams on the Pull Out Pattern Sheet.

Preparation

1 Using the marker pen, trace the placement diagram from the pattern sheet. Cut a 36 cm (14½ in) square from the background fabric. Tape the tracing to a light box or a window in daylight and tape the fabric square over the top. Lightly trace the design onto the fabric, just inside the tracing lines so the pencil lines will be hidden under appliqué pieces.

2 Make templates for all the pattern pieces.

3 There are several methods for appliqué and the method you choose will affect the way you cut out and prepare the appliqué pieces:

If you intend to use 'needle-turn' appliqué, draw the pattern pieces onto the right side of the fabric with a 3 mm (⅛ in) seam allowance.

If you intend to use freezer paper or baste onto cardboard, draw the pattern pieces onto the right side of the fabric with a 6 mm (¼ in) seam allowance.

Appliqué

Following the numbers on the placement diagram for the order, appliqué the pieces into place, using your chosen method, overlapping them as shown and attaching all the **D** leaves last of all. Don't attach the flower centres **G** and **H** at this stage.

Embroidery

Embroider the stems in stem stitch, using two strands of embroidery floss.

Finishing

Assemble the quilt sandwich. Sew the buttons onto the pansies, then sew on the flower centres **G** and **H**.

Have your picture framed as we have done or make it up into a pretty cushion.

The Sisters

MADE BY PAT PALMER, CALIFORNIA

These saucy sisters will add cheer to any wall in your home.

Finished size: 102 cm x 104 cm (40 in x 41 in)

Materials

- 🍀 fabric for the dolls, clothes, wings, boots, hair
- 🍀 two fabrics for the borders
- 🍀 112 cm (44 in) square of fabric for the backing
- 🍀 80 cm (32 in) of fabric for the background
- 🍀 112 cm (44 in) square of Pellon or Rayfelt
- 🍀 scraps of lace
- 🍀 fourteen small buttons
- 🍀 two buttons or beads
- 🍀 pinking shears
- 🍀 Pigma pens or fabric marker pens
- 🍀 dark quilting thread, Burgundy or Navy
- 🍀 hank of Perle Cotton
- 🍀 template plastic
- 🍀 small piece of cardboard
- 🍀 black fineline permanent marker pen
- 🍀 piece of old sock or sweater
- 🍀 polyester fibre fill

Method

See the Templates on the Pull Out Pattern Sheet.

Preparation

Trace the templates and cut them out of the template plastic. Add 6 mm ($1/4$ in) seam allowances all around when cutting the pieces from the fabric.

For the background

1 Cut the following: a piece 74 cm x 76 cm (29 in x 30 in) from the background fabric; four 5 cm (2 in) wide strips from the first border fabric; four 11 cm ($4^{1/4}$ in) wide strips from the second border fabric.

2 Measure in 19 cm ($7^{1/2}$ in) from both sides of the background piece. Press along these lines to mark the placement for the dolls.

3 Measure 11.5 cm ($4^{1/2}$ in) from the top of the background piece. Press along this line to mark the placement of the dolls' heads.

For the arms and legs

1 Cut out four leg, four arm, four boot and four hand pieces for each doll. Sew the boots to the legs and the hands to the arms. Press the seam allowances open.

2 Using a small machine stitch and with the right sides together, join the pieces together in pairs, leaving the top edges open. Clip carefully into the curves and turn the pieces through to the right side.

3 Fill the hands/arms softly with the fibre fill up to the last 1 cm ($3/8$ in). Stitch the fingers either by hand or by machine. Fill the legs softly one-third of the way up the leg. Tie a knot for the knee, then continue to fill up to 1 cm ($3/8$ in) from the top.

For the wings

Cut eight wing shapes roughly from fabric and four from Pellon or Rayfelt. Place the wing shapes together in pairs with the Pellon or Rayfelt in between. Quilt the outline of the wings, using the dark thread, then cut out the wings to the actual shape, using the pinking shears. Baste the wings into position on the background fabric.

For the head

Cut out the fabric for the head, then trace the face outline onto the fabric, using the Pigma pens or the marker pens. Baste the fabric over a cardboard template, then press it well to ensure the curves are smooth. Remove the template and appliqué the head into position.

For the body

1 Pin the arms and legs into position with the seams to the centre front and back.

2 Baste, then appliqué the body into position over the arms and legs making sure that the stitching is secure and goes

right through all thicknesses of fabric, especially over the arms and legs.

For the skirt

1 Cut a 24 cm x 28 cm (9½ in x 11 in) fabric piece for the skirt. Stitch a small hem down the sides and across the bottom, then attach a length of lace at the bottom edge.

2 Turn over 1 cm (³/8 in) at the top edge of the skirt. Sew two rows of gathering along the top edge. Pull up the gathering so the waist is 11.5 cm (4½ in). Stitch the skirt onto the doll, sewing a length of ungathered lace along the waist at the same time.

3 Stitch lace around the sleeve ends to make a cuff and across the neck to make a collar.

To complete Sister 1

1 Cut twenty to twenty-four 1 cm x 6 cm (³/8 in x 2³/8 in) strips of the hair fabric. Stitch these flat around the head. Stitch twelve of the small buttons onto the head to cover the hair ends.

2 Stitch the hands together, then stitch them to the bodice in a praying position.

To complete Sister 2

1 Cut off approximately 1 m (1¹/8 yd) of Perle Cotton for the boot laces. Twist the remainder of the hank so that it covers the top of the doll's head and stitch it into position with a matching thread. Cut a 4 cm x 40 cm (1½ in x 15³/4 in) strip of the second border fabric and tie it into a bow. Sew the bow into place.

2 Stitch the hands together holding the basket.

Finishing

1 Cut out small pieces of fabric with the pinking shears. Write on them with the Pigma pens or the marker pens. Stitch the tags onto the top of the dolls' legs.

2 Cut the backing fabric and the Pellon or Rayfelt a little larger than the quilt top. Assemble the quilt sandwich, then quilt the wallhanging in a design that pleases you. Ours has been quilted in sunflowers, crows and birdhouses – mirroring the design on the fabrics.

3 Cut four 5.5 cm (2¹/4 in) wide strips. Fold them over double with the wrong sides together. Stitch the binding to the right sides of the sides of the wallhanging with the raw edges even. Turn the binding to the back of the wallhanging and slipstitch it into place. Bind the top and the bottom in the same way.

4 Cut the socks from the piece of old sock or sweater and stitch them around the legs.

5 Using the Perle Cotton, make boot laces for Sister 1. Stitch the two buttons or beads onto the shoes of Sister 2 and two remaining small buttons on her dress bodice.

6 Stitch a casing to the back of the quilt and hang your quilt so the Sisters can watch over you.

Violet Time

MADE BY FAY KING

Embroidered hand towels are always popular, and this pretty violet design is sure to please.

Materials

- ❧ hand towel
- ❧ DMC Stranded Cotton: Purple, Peach, Green, Yellow
- ❧ Piecemakers milliners or straw needles, sizes 3-9
- ❧ Piecemakers between needle, size 9
- ❧ 20 cm (8 in) of white Swiss voile
- ❧ 20 cm (8 in) of iron-on Vilene, medium weight
- ❧ guipure lace edging
- ❧ spray starch
- ❧ small embroidery hoop 10-12.5 cm (4-5 in)
- ❧ H pencil

Method

See the Embroidery Design below.

Preparation

1 Cut a length of voile 5 cm (2 in) wider than the towel. Spray well with the spray starch, then iron.

2 Lay the voile over the pattern and, using the pencil, trace the bows and leaves onto the right side of the fabric.

Embroidery

1 Place the fabric into the embroidery hoop and make sure it is held very tightly. Work the shadow embroidery in one strand of Peach, using the between needle and working from the front of the work. Embroider the bow loops first, then the tails. Outline the leaves in stem stitch, using one strand of Green and the between needle.

2 Work the violets, using three strands of cotton and the size 7 milliners or straw needle. Note that the violet has five petals which should be worked in the same order for each flower.

3 When the embroidery is completed, spray the piece again with the starch and press well, taking care not to press on the violets but bring the point of the iron in around them.

Finishing

1 Lay the embroidery face down on a soft towel. Cut the Vilene 6 cm (2¼ in) wide and the length of the towel width. Find the centre of the Vilene and match it to the centre of the embroidery. Iron it into place.

2 Trim the voile so that it is 12 mm (½ in) larger all around than the Vilene. Press the seam allowance firmly to the back.

3 Pin, then baste the embroidered piece onto the towel. Stitch it into place, either by machine or by hand.

4 Cut the guipure lace edging 12 mm (½ in) wider than the towel. Hand roll and stitch a small 6 mm (¼ in) hem at each end, then stitch the edging to the edge of the towel using a straight stitch and a small zigzag.

Stitch Guide

Shadow embroidery

1 Run the thread through the fabric approximately 1 cm (³/₈ in) from the end leaving a tail of thread on the front. This will be cut off later. Make sure the stitches are tiny and that the bulk of the stitch is on the back (Fig. 1).

2 Bring the needle to the front approximately 3 mm (¹/₈ in) from the end of the point (Fig. 2) and make a back stitch (Fig. 3).

3 Come up 3 mm (¹/₈ in) from the point on the other side and stitch a back stitch (Fig. 4), travel to the first side and stitch a back stitch (Fig. 5). This will create a herringbone on the back of your work (Fig. 6).

4 When you have completed the area or you are running short of thread, run the thread along the back edge of the work and snip it off. Begin again as before.

Violets

1 Take a small stitch so the thread and the needle point are together (Fig. 7). Twist the thread thirty-two times around the needle (Fig. 8). Take the threads off the needle and ease it so that all the loops are even. Take the thread to the back. Shape the loop into an oval, not a circle (Fig. 9).

2 Work thirty-two twists for Loop 2. Work eighteen twists on both Loops 3 and 4. Loop 5 sits over Loop 3 and 4 and has twenty-five twists (Fig. 10).

3 The centre is a small bullion of eight twists, approximately 2 mm (¹/₁₆ in) long, placed over the ends of each of the others.

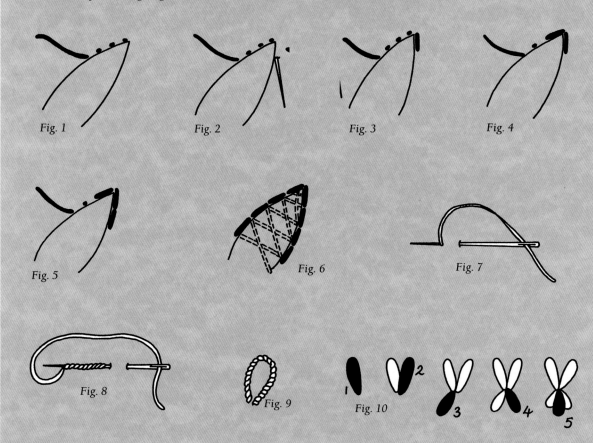

Fig. 1　　Fig. 2　　Fig. 3　　Fig. 4

Fig. 5　　Fig. 6　　Fig. 7

Fig. 8　　Fig. 9　　Fig. 10

Victorian Sewing Box

MADE BY WENDY LEE RAGAN, FLORIDA

If you have no need for a beautiful sewing box, this embroidery design is very suitable for pillows and linens for the home and selected motifs are ideal for collars and dresses.

Note: Each monogram will fit into the same area as the R on the pattern square. Please add your own finishing touches to individualise your initial.

Materials

- ❧ 46 cm (18 in) square of Ulster Weavers 14HC white linen
- ❧ mahogany sewing box
- ❧ DMC Stranded Cotton: White, Light Yellow, Green, Pink, Light Pink, Light Blue, Blue
- ❧ DMC 50 cotton thread, White, as the couching thread for the appliqué cord and fil tiré
- ❧ embroidery hoop
- ❧ needles
- ❧ spray starch
- ❧ tracing paper
- ❧ pencil
- ❧ water-soluble marker pen

Method

See the Embroidery Design and the Monogram Alphabet on the Pull Out Pattern Sheet.

1 Pull threads on the linen to square it up, then spray the linen with starch.

2 Trace the embroidery design from the pattern sheet and transfer it to the linen, using the marker pen. Trace the monogram you need and transfer that into the centre of the design. An easy way to manage this is to tape the tracing to a window in daylight and tape the linen over the top. This way you can quite simply trace the design onto the linen. Take care to use very light markings and test your marker pen on a scrap of fabric first to make sure it will wash out.

3 Secure the linen in the embroidery hoop and embroider the design, following the stitch guide and the colour key.

Stitch Guide

Shadow embroidery

Use a crewel needle, size 10, and a 45 cm/18 in single strand of stranded embroidery cotton. Place the fabric in a hoop and begin with a waste knot. In shadow stitch, you form a basketweave of thread that covers the area to be filled and is surrounded by back stitches.

1 Bring the needle through at **a** and take a stitch to **b**. Bring the needle up at **c** and take a stitch to **b**. (Fig. A)

2 Bring the needle up at **d** and take a stitch to **a**. On the wrong side, carry the thread over, bringing it out at **e** and take a stitch to **c**. (Fig. B)

3 On the wrong side, carry the thread over, bringing it out at **f** then take a stitch back to **d**. On the wrong side, carry the thread over, bringing it out at **g** then take a stitch back to **e**. Continue in this way until the area is filled. (Fig. C)

Granitos or rondels

These are tiny dots made by laying six or seven straight stitches over one another. They can be worked with or without a hoop.

Split stitch

This is commonly used for padding which is covered by other stitches. It can be worked with or without a hoop. (Fig. D)

Bullion stitches

Bullion stitches are the basis for many flowers.

1 Begin by anchoring the thread, then take a stitch from **a** to **b**, taking the needle back to **a**. Insert the needle at **b** again, just up to the eye. (Fig. E)

2 Wrap the thread around the needle, keeping it close to **a**. (Fig. F). Controlling the wraps firmly with your left thumb, push the needle through and slide the wraps off the needle. Slide the wraps down the thread until they are lying on the fabric. Reinsert the needle at **b**.
Bullion rosebuds are made by laying two bullion stitches side by side. Make one of the bullions one wrap larger than the other. For a bullion rose, make three bullions side by side. The inside one is usually one or two wraps smaller than the outside ones. Here's a tip: wrap the thread around the needle until the tube is the desired length, then add one more wrap. This is to compensate for the fact that the bullion will compact when you slide it off the needle.

For bullion pinwheels, draw a circle of the desired size with a dot in the centre. Stitch around the outside with split stitches, then make bullions from the outside ring, over the split stitches, into the centre, until the circle is filled.

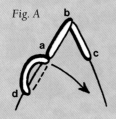

Fig. A

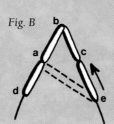

Fig. B

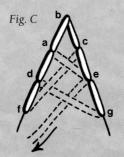

Fig. C

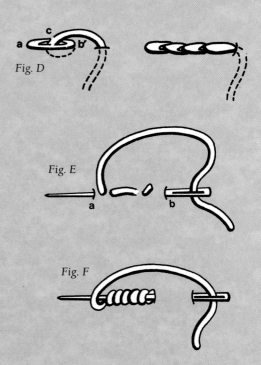

Fig. D

Fig. E

Fig. F

Shaded eyelets

1 Draw an oval with an offset circle inside it. Outline both with split stitches. (Fig. G) With an awl, push open the threads inside the circle. Don't break the threads.

2 Inside the oval, stitch two or three layers of padding satin stitches, alternating the direction of the layers. (Fig. H)

3 When the padding is completed, satin stitch around the eyelet over the padding. These shaded eyelets can be stitched with or without a hoop. (Fig. J)

Appliqué cord

1 Cut a length of cord (stranded cotton) that is twice the length of the outline. Anchor the cord in the fabric.

2 Pinstitch over the cord until you have completed the outline. (Fig. K)

3 Bring the cord around and pinstitch over it, working back the way you came, but on the other side and using the same holes. (Fig. L)

4 To finish, overlap the cords and couch them, or bring them to the back of your work and tie them off or weave them into the stitches.

Fil tiré

1 Start with a waste knot. Stitch from **A** to **B**. Repeat. Bring the needle up at **C**. Stitch from **C** to **D**. Repeat, bringing the needle up at **E**. Turn the work upside down (like smocking) and repeat the steps above, from right to left, stitching in the previous holes where necessary. Continue until your design is filled (Figs M and N).

2 Turn the work ninety degrees. Stitch the horizontal lines in the same way as the vertical lines, using the same holes. End by weaving the thread on the back of the work (Figs O and P).

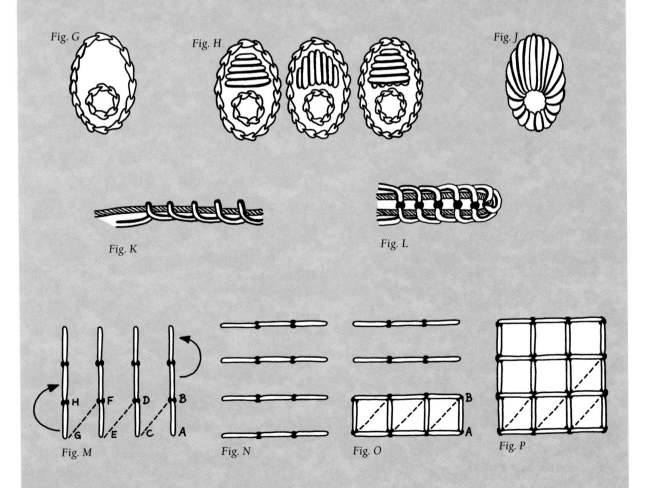

Fig. G   Fig. H   Fig. J

Fig. K   Fig. L

Fig. M   Fig. N   Fig. O   Fig. P

Petit Point Brooch

STITCHED BY AILSA CARADUS, NEW ZEALAND

Ailsa specialises in miniatures and has designed this pretty brooch especially for us.

Note: This piece could also be worked on linen, working over two threads, or on Aida cloth, using cross stitch.

Materials

- ♣ DMC Stranded Cotton in the colours indicated
- ♣ 5 cm (2 in) square of 40-count silk gauze
- ♣ scraps of homespun
- ♣ 10 cm (4 in) embroidery hoop
- ♣ Piecemakers crewel needle, size 10
- ♣ purchased brooch and fittings

Method

See the Embroidery Design below.

Preparation

1 Finger press the silk gauze square into quarters to find the centre. Mark the fold with lines of running stitch.

2 Stitch the homespun scraps to the edges of the silk gauze to allow it to be fitted into the embroidery hoop. Place the piece in the hoop so the square of silk is centred, straight and absolutely square.

3 Blunt the needle, using an emery board.

Embroidery

1 Embroider the rose design, following the chart and the colour key, using one strand of cotton.

2 When the embroidery is completed, remove the basting and the pieces of homespun.

Finishing

Fit the embroidery into the brooch frame, following the manufacturer's instructions.

Colour Key

ROSE	■	Black
	oo / oo	902
	\\ / \\	326
	— / —	891
	•• / ••	3706
LEAVES	◤ / ◣	935
	XX / XX	470
	ℓℓ / ℓℓ	840

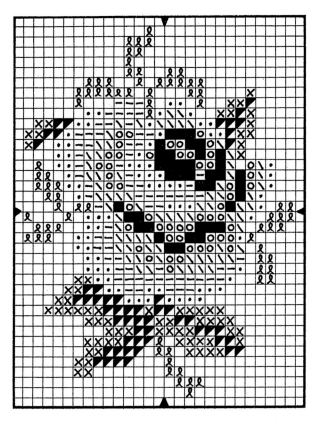

Matrioshki Doll

MADE BY MARIA KIRK, ENGLAND

This exquisite embroidered doll was inspired by traditional Russian dolls and would be a delight to own or give as a gift.

Materials

- ♣ 23 cm x 25.5 cm (9 in x 10 in) piece of black heavy silk fabric
- ♣ 15 cm x 17.5 cm (6 in x 7 in) piece of wine-coloured silk fabric
- ♣ two 4 cm (1½ in) diameter cardboard circles
- ♣ 4 m (4½ yd) of 4 mm (³/₁₆ in) wide silk ribbon: Rich Purple, Green, Burgundy, Antique Gold
- ♣ spool of thread, Gold
- ♣ 2 m (2¼ yd) of fine gold cord
- ♣ wadding
- ♣ viscose or mohair for the hair
- ♣ Doll's House ¹/₁₂ scale doll's head on a shoulder plate
- ♣ craft glue
- ♣ strong thread
- ♣ tacky craft glue (optional)

Method

The skirt

See the Pattern and the Embroidery Design on page 29.

1 Fold over and baste the edges of the black fabric to prevent them fraying. Finger-press the fabric in half, then in half again. Baste along the fold lines to mark the fabric into quarters.

2 Using one of the lines of basting as a guide for the centre front of the skirt, embroider the skirt design, following the embroidery design on the pattern.

3 Using the strong thread and running stitch, gather the edge of the circle. Pull up the gathering until the fabric forms a ball, then stuff it firmly with the wadding until you have a nice rounded shape.

4 Attach the head to the top of the skirt ball, slipping the shoulders inside and making sure the face is lined up level with the embroidery. Tie off the gathering threads to close the ball.

For the headscarf

1 Using a running stitch, sew the two scarf pieces together around the curved edge. Turn the scarf to the right side. Carefully turn in the raw straight edges. Whipstitch the edges together neatly.

2 Following the embroidery design, work the embroidery around the scarf. Work the edging by couching the gold cord down with the Gold thread.

Finishing

1 Glue the hair neatly onto the head with a little glue, taking care not to place it too far down over the forehead. Take the excess hair around to the back of the head and glue it down neatly.

2 Making sure the top embroidery on the headscarf is centred, dab a little glue on the top of the head and carefully stick down the headscarf. Hold it in place with pins, while you adjust it to your liking, then sew it in place. Carefully stitch the ends of the headscarf together under the chin, using a little glue if necessary to hold it, then, as neatly as possible, sew the headscarf to the skirt. If you wish, you can use a tacky fabric glue to help hold the scarf.

3 Cover the two cardboard discs with the black fabric by turning the fabric edge over the card and gluing it in place. Glue both card discs together, then whipstitch them together. Pin the gold cord around the edge, then couch it in place with the Gold thread. Finally, glue the disc to the base of the skirt ball, making sure the doll is well balanced.

Note: To make your doll a little special, try adding a few drops of potpourri oil to the stuffing of the skirt – but take care not to get any on the fabric – or you can use her as a special pin or needle cushion.

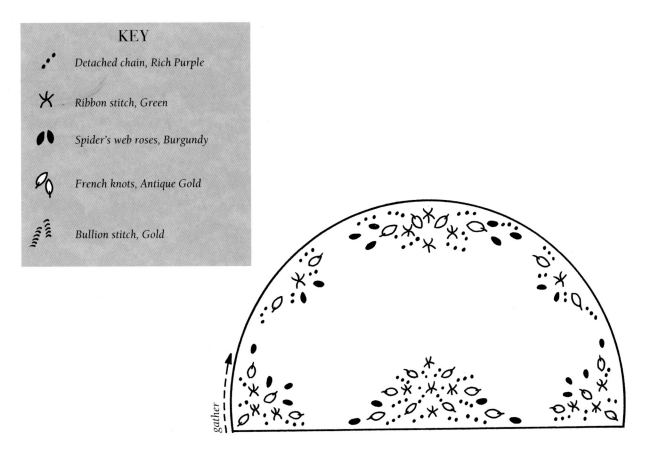

KEY

⠒	*Detached chain, Rich Purple*
✳	*Ribbon stitch, Green*
◖◗	*Spider's web roses, Burgundy*
◊	*French knots, Antique Gold*
〰	*Bullion stitch, Gold*

gather

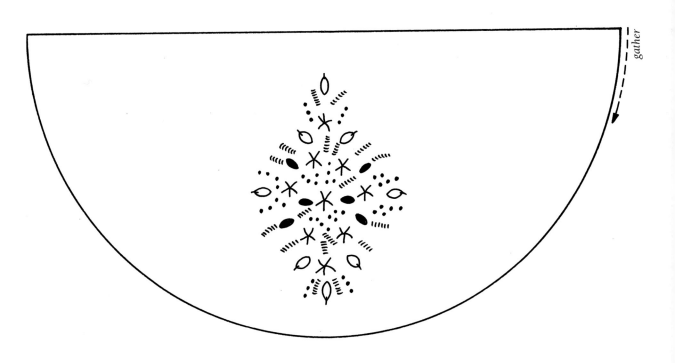

gather

Continental Pillow Covers

MADE BY MARLENE BURIAN, CALIFORNIA

These elegant pillow covers will add a touch of luxury to a beautiful boudoir, especially when they are personalised with a silk-ribbon-embroidered monogram.

Finished size: 60 cm (24 in) square

Materials

- ❧ **1.8 m (2 yd) of grosgrain embossed fabric (this will make two pillow covers)**
- ❧ **2 m (2¼ yd) of piping cord**
- ❧ **Kanagawa Silk Twist: Green, Mauve, Grey**
- ❧ **1 m (1¼ yd) each of 4 mm (3/16 in) wide silk ribbon: Deep Pink, Dusty Pink, Pink, Pale Pink, Cream**
- ❧ **tapestry needles, size 24**
- ❧ **water-soluble marker pen**

Note: Always check that the marker pen will wash out by testing it on the fabric edge before using it on your project.

Method

See the Alphabet and the Embroidery Designs on the Pull Out Pattern Sheet.

Cutting

Cut the following from the fabric: two 25 cm (10 in) squares, two pieces 33.5 cm x 62 cm (13 in x 24½ in), two pieces 45 cm x 62 cm (17¾ in x 24½ in) and eight strips 20 cm x 25 cm (7⅞ in x 10 in). Cut two strips 3 cm x 115 cm (1¼ in x 45 in) for the piping.

Embroidery

Using the marker pen, mark your chosen initials in the centre of the fabric squares. Embroider the initials, following the embroidery designs.

Assembling

1 Join the strips for the piping. Lay the piping cord along the centre of the wrong side of the fabric strip. Fold the strip over, enclosing the cord and stitch as close as possible to the cord, using the zipper foot on your machine.

2 For each pillow, cut the piping into four 25 cm (10 in) lengths. Lay one on each edge of the fabric square with the raw edges even. Using the zipper foot, stitch on the piping.

3 Find the centre point of the 20 cm (7⅞ in) wide strips and stitch one strip to each side of the square, matching the centre of the strip to the centre of the side of the square, beginning and ending 6 mm (¼ in) from the corner.

4 To mitre the corners, lay the embroidered piece on the table with the edging strips lying flat. Fold the ends of the top and bottom strips under so that they lie exactly over the side strips. Pin the mitres to hold them in position, then slipstitch or machine-stitch them into position. Trim the ends to make them square.

5 On the 45 cm x 62 cm (17¾ in x 24 in) pieces of fabric, fold a 1 cm (3/8 in) hem on one long edge, then fold another 2.5 cm (1 in) hem. Stitch the hem.

6 With the right sides together, lay the short back piece, then the longer back piece over the pillow front with the hemmed edges overlapping in the centre. Stitch around the outer edge, using a 1 cm (3/8 in) seam allowance. Stitch in slightly at each corner. Turn the pillow cover to the right side.

Autumn Glow

MADE BY GLORIA McKINNON

Bring the style of the Victorian era to your home with this beautiful picture using 'antique' velvet flowers, berries and leaves.

Materials

- ♣ 70 cm (28 in) of cream Dupion silk
- ♣ 70 cm (28 in) square of Rayfelt
- ♣ 25 cm (10 in) of Liberty fabric for the appliqué
- ♣ 20 cm (8 in) of contrasting fabric for the appliqué
- ♣ cotton thread in a neutral colour
- ♣ Piecemaker crewel needles, size 8
- ♣ water-soluble marker pen
- ♣ tracing paper
- ♣ pencil
- ♣ cardboard for templates
- ♣ quilting frame
- ♣ ordinary sewing cotton to match the appliqué fabric
- ♣ two or three large antique velvet berries
- ♣ three stems of antique velvet pussy willow
- ♣ three stems of antique velvet green leaves with gold tips
- ♣ five stems of orange pansies
- ♣ five stems of purple pansies
- ♣ five stems of burgundy pansies
- ♣ five stems of ivory pansies
- ♣ old scissors or wire cutters

Method

See the Urn Pattern on the Pull Out Pattern Sheet.

Preparation

Cut a 70 cm (28 in) square of the silk fabric and overlock or zigzag the edges to prevent fraying. Mark the centre line of the piece and another line 20 cm (8 in) from the bottom edge. This is the placement line for the base of the urn.

Appliqué

1 Trace the urn pattern. Make templates from the cardboard. Using the templates, cut out the fabric pieces allowing a 6 mm (1/4 in) seam allowance all around.

2 Carefully baste the fabric onto the templates, clipping the curves, where necessary, to create smooth curves. Do not clip too deeply or the fabric will fray. Press the pieces well so that the curves will be permanent, using the point of your iron on the wrong side of the fabric and pushing in from the edge to remove any small fabric points. Remove the basting and slip the cardboard out.

3 Baste the pieces into position, then appliqué, using a blind hem stitch. Use a thread colour that matches the piece that you are appliquéing.

For the flowers

1 Baste the 70 cm (28 in) square of Rayfelt behind the fabric, basting the sides first, then the top and bottom. This way it will stay flat and square.

2 Lay the gold-tipped stems and pussy willow stems onto your fabric in a pleasing background arrangement. Note that there must be adequate height – the arrangement should be at least twice the height of the urn and it should extend approximately one urn width to each side, so that the arrangement is well balanced.

3 When you have your background leaves in position, mark under the tips of the outermost leaves with a dot, using the water-soluble marker pen.

4 Place your piece firmly and evenly into the quilting frame so that you can work on your piece with both hands. Working from the outer edges to the centre, stitch the stems, catching them in enough places to hold them securely in place.

5 Start placing the pansies from the outside working towards the centre. You will need to cut each pansy stem to approximately 12 mm (1/2 in) in length, using the old scissors or wire cutters.

6 Stitch the flowers down from behind, catching down each stem and stitching through the base of the back petals of each flower. Make sure all the flowers and leaves are secure. Stitch the antique berries into any spaces.

Roses and Lilacs Tea Cosy

MADE BY FAY KING

Add an elegant touch to tea time with this pretty wool-embroidered tea cosy.

Materials

- ❧ 30 cm x 80 cm (12 in x 32 in) of cream wool blanketing
- ❧ 50 cm (20 in) of printed floral fabric for the lining and the frill
- ❧ Appleton's Crewel Wool: three shades of Lilac, two shades of Rose, Yellow, White, Green, Beige
- ❧ Piecemakers tapestry needles, size 22
- ❧ 50 cm (20 in) of 7 mm (5/16 in) wide silk ribbon, Dusty Pink
- ❧ tracing paper
- ❧ black fineline permanent marker pen
- ❧ water-soluble marker pen (optional)
- ❧ pencil

Method

See the Pattern and the Embroidery Design on the Pull Out Pattern Sheet.

1 Using the pattern provided, cut two tea cosy shapes from the wool blanketing.

2 Trace the embroidery design onto the tracing paper. Cut out the shape and use this to mark the teapot outline onto the blanketing, using either a light pencil line or the water-soluble marker pen. Mark the position of the roses and the bow onto the teapot. **Note:** it is important to match the crosses marked on the design and on the background.

Embroidery

Embroider the teapot outline, using a small stem stitch and pink crewel wool. Remember always to keep the thread to the outside of the curve to give you a smooth, even curve.

For the roses

Embroider the four roses first, following the guide below and using two strands of Appleton's wool.

For the lilacs

Embroider very small lazy daisy flowers for the lilacs. Each flower has five petals. Start from the top of the flower and work to the tip, grading the colour from dark to light.

For the daisies

Using one strand of White wool, stitch lazy daisy stitches with a one-strand Yellow French knot centre. Trail White French knots from the flowers.

For the leaves

Stitch the leaves in detached chain stitch, using one strand of Green.

Rose

Using the darker Rose tapestry wool, make four straight stitches, then make another four over the top to form the padded raised centre.

Change to the lighter Rose wool and stitch around the centre as illustrated. The stitches should lie gently over the edges of the centre. Turn your work a quarter turn each time, until all four sides are completed.

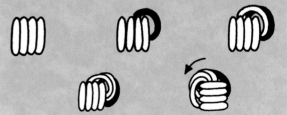

For the bow

Tie the silk ribbon into a bow and stitch it into position, below the roses. Thread the ends into the needle and thread them through the blanketing to the back.

Finishing

1 With the right sides together, stitch around the curved edge of the tea cosy pieces, using a 1 cm (³⁄8 in) seam.

2 Cut two strips of lining fabric, each 7.5 cm x 72 cm (3 in x 28 in). Stitch the short ends together to make a loop. Fold the loop over double with the wrong sides together. Gather the raw edges with two rows of gathering stitches. Pull up the gathering to fit around the base of the tea cosy, matching seams to seams then, with the raw edges matching, stitch the frill onto the right side of the blanketing.

3 Cut two tea cosy shapes from the lining fabric. Join them with the right sides together, leaving a 10 cm (4 in) opening at the top as marked on the pattern.

4 Pull the lining over the blanketing so that the right sides are together. Stitch them together around the base. Turn the tea cosy right side out through the opening in the lining. Slipstitch the opening closed and push the lining up into the tea cosy.

Drunkard's Path Quilt

MADE BY DIANA MARKS, CALIFORNIA

This quilt is a great way to use up your scraps or charm pieces you have been collecting.

Diana had been collecting off-white fabrics when she won the fat quarter lottery in the craft forum on Compuserve. These 'on-line' quilters come from all over the world, including Australia.

There are many different ways of constructing Drunkard's Path. Some methods require pins, some clipping, some use freezer paper. We have found Anita Murphy's pinless technique to be the easiest and fastest.

We wish to thank Chitra Publications, publishers of *Traditional Quiltworks* for allowing us to reproduce the quilt made by Lynn Mann.

Finished size: 137 cm x 165 cm (54 in x 66 in)

Materials

- ♣ 7.5 cm (3 in) Drunkard's Path templates
- ♣ 3.6 m (4 yd) total of different lights/neutrals
- ♣ 1.83 m (2 yd) total of different darks
- ♣ 1.14 m (1¼ yd) of dark fabric for the border and binding
- ♣ 3.6 m (4 yd) of fabric for the backing
- ♣ 147 cm x 175 cm (58 in x 60 in) of wadding
- ♣ 15 cm (6 in) bias square
- ♣ small rotary cutter
- ♣ small and large self-healing cutting mats

Method

Cutting

Note: The plastic templates are full size and include the 6 mm (¼ in) seam allowance. Use the small rotary cutter to cut around the template keeping the rotary cutter straight. If you cut on the small mat it will be easier to turn as you are cutting.

1 Cut one 11.5 cm (4½ in) strip from each of your scraps. If you are using charm pieces, 12.7 cm (5 in) or 15 cm (6 in) pieces will be fine. Do not cut these into strips. You will also need some 14 cm (5½ in) strips from your lights for the border, so don't cut everything.

2 Cut the following pieces:
48 A from the light scraps;

240 A from the medium or dark scraps;

48 B from the medium or dark scraps;

240 B from the light scraps; and

96 C from the light scraps for the border. Piece these to make twenty-four 14 cm (5½ in) squares, then cut them all from corner to corner in both directions.

3 Cut three 4 cm x 114 cm (1⅝ in x 44 in) dark solid strips and nine 5 cm x 114 cm (2 in x 44 in) dark solid strips for the borders.

4 Cut six 7.5 cm x 114 cm (3 in x 44 in) dark solid strips for the binding.

Piecing

1 Place an L-shaped piece on top of a pie-shaped piece, with the right sides together (Fig. 1). Take no more than three or four stitches, very slowly. Leaving your needle in the fabric, bring the L-shaped piece back over the pie-shaped piece with the raw edges matching (Fig. 2). Continue in this way, making sure you have an accurate 6 mm (¼ in) seam allowance. Do not be alarmed if the bottom edges do not match up perfectly. Press the seam allowance towards the pie-shaped piece. You can use your bias square to even out your pieces to 9 cm (3½ in) squares before joining them into rows. As you become more comfortable with the technique, you can begin chain-piecing.

2 Take four Drunkard's Path squares with light As and twelve with dark As (Figs 3 and 4). Arrange them as shown, with the light As in the corners (Fig. 5). Stitch the squares into rows, then stitch the rows together to complete one block.

3 Lay the blocks out in four rows of three blocks each. Sew the blocks together into rows, then sew the rows together to complete the quilt top.

For the borders

1 Centre and stitch a 2.5 cm x 114 cm (1 in x 44 in) dark solid strip to the top and bottom of the quilt.

2 Take the three 4 cm x 114 cm (1⅝ in x 44 in) dark solid strips. Cut one in half and sew the two halves to the other two pieces. Then centre and sew these strips to the left and right sides of the quilt.

3 Take fifteen Drunkard's Path squares and fifteen of the light scrap triangles. Arrange them as shown in figure 6. You can stitch the squares and triangles together by working in diagonal rows. Make a second border like the first one.

4 Sew the border units to the top and bottom edges of the quilt, positioning each border unit with its longer side touching the dark solid border.

5 Take twenty-one Drunkard's Path squares and twenty-one light scrap triangles. Arrange them in a border unit similar to the ones you've already stitched, but instead of having nine triangles along the longer side, there will be twelve. Make a second border unit the same.

6 Sew the border units to the left and right sides of the quilt. Again, position them so that their longer side is against the dark solid border.

7 Arrange six Drunkard's Path squares and six light scrap triangles as shown in figure 7. Stitch them together, making a corner unit for the border. Make four corner units

in the same way. Join one to each corner of the quilt.

8 Take four of the 5 cm (2 in) wide dark solid strips and sew them together in pairs. Centre and sew these to the left and right sides of the quilt.

9 Take four more of the 5 cm (2 in) wide strips and sew them in pairs. Cut the remaining 5 cm (2 in) wide strip in half and sew half to each pair.

Quilting

1 Press the quilt top well. Assemble the quilt sandwich, then baste through all thicknesses with lines of stitching approximately 10 cm (4 in) apart.

2 Quilt in a design of your choice – this quilt requires little more than outline quilting.

Binding

Fold the binding strips over double with the wrong sides together. Stitch the binding to the right side of the sides of the quilt with the raw edges matching. Turn the binding to the back of the quilt and slipstitch it into place. Bind the top and the bottom in the same way.

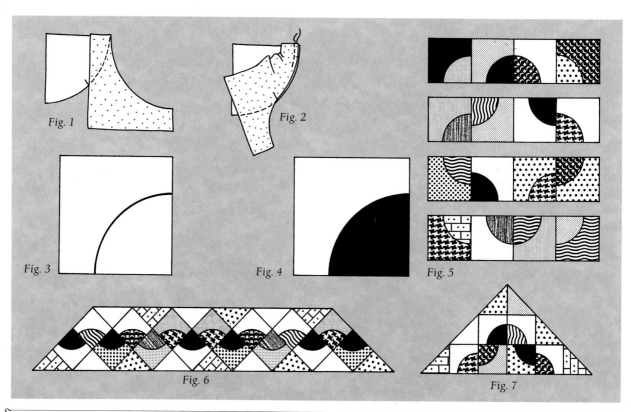

Fig. 1 Fig. 2 Fig. 3 Fig. 4 Fig. 5 Fig. 6 Fig. 7

Lace Flower Basket

MADE BY GLORIA MCKINNON

A pretty lace basket adorns this wonderful knee rug for your favourite aunt or family member.

Materials

- ❧ 80 cm x 115 cm (32 in x 45 in) piece of cream wool blanketing
- ❧ 1 m (1¹/₈ yd) of fabric for the backing
- ❧ DMC Tapestry Wool: Dark Dusty Pink, Medium Dusty Pink, Light Dusty Pink, Medium Pink, Light Pink, Ecru
- ❧ Appleton's Crewel Wool: Mauve, Deep Mauve, Blue, Yellow, Medium Lilac, Light Lilac, Apricot, Blue/Green, Grey/Green, Deep Blue Green, Medium Plum, Pink
- ❧ Au Ver a Soie: Cream, Pale Pink
- ❧ ordinary sewing thread, Cream
- ❧ 1 m (1¹/₈ yd) of 4 mm (³/₁₆ in) wide silk ribbon, Green
- ❧ 25 cm (10 in) of 12.5 cm (4¹/₂ in) wide Swiss needlerun lace for the basket
- ❧ 15 cm (6 in) of cream lawn
- ❧ 4 m (4¹/₂ yd) of cream lace edging
- ❧ tracing paper
- ❧ pencil

Method

See the Basket Pattern and the Embroidery Design on the Pull Out Pattern Sheet.

1 Using the pattern provided, cut the cream lawn to the basket shape.

2 Lay the lace over the lawn, fold the lace edges around the lawn and baste them together.

3 Mark the position of the basket on the blanket wool, placing the lip of the basket 4 cm (1¹/₂ in) below the centre point of the blanket. Appliqué the basket into position.

Embroidery

1 Mark an arc on the blanket that rises to approximately 15 cm (6 in) above the top of the basket and extends 5 cm (2 in) on either side of it. Embroider the flowers massed within this arc, but don't be too rigid – allow some of the flowers to extend beyond the line.

2 Work the dark centre roses, using the three shades of Dusty Pink tapestry wool. Work the centre in the darkest shade, then the medium and finally the lightest shade. The other roses are worked in two shades of pink. Always use the darker colour for the centre.

3 Work the lilac roses with a centre of seven colonial knots in two strands of the darker lilac and the outer rounds in the lighter lilac.

4 Embroider the large daisies in Ecru tapestry wool with Yellow French knot centres and the smaller daisies in Medium Plum and Pink wool with Yellow or Dark Dusty Pink centres.

5 Embroider the buttonhole wheels in Blue, Mauve or Pink wool.

6 Embroider the wisteria in French knots in Lilac wool. Embroider the buds in trails, using the deeper pink wool.

7 Embroider the lavender in bullion knots, using two strands of Mauve wool – each with eight twists.

8 Scatter ribbon roses throughout the arrangement, including a few on the lace with small buds and leaves in Green silk ribbon straight stitch.

9 Using the Pale Pink and Cream silk threads, embroider daisies scattered among the flowers.

10 Fill the spaces with Blue French knot forget-me-nots with Yellow French knot centres.

11 Scatter heather among the roses, using two strands of Medium Plum or Pink, making bullions with eight twists. Embroider the centre first and then place two bullions on either side.

12 Using two different greens, scatter lazy daisy stitch leaves among the flowers.

Finishing

1 Cut the backing fabric to the exact size of the blanket piece. Lay the backing fabric face down on a table with the blanket, face up, on top. Baste them together, working from the centre to the edges and from the centre to the corners.

2 Lay the lace on the blanket edge, so that 2 cm (³/4 in) extends beyond the blanket edge. Fold the corners of the lace into mitres. Pin the mitres carefully. Lift the lace off the blanket and stitch the mitres on the wrong side of the lace. Trim away the excess lace behind the mitres. Replace the lace on the blanket and baste it into place. The corners will sit exactly on the blanket corners. The 2 cm (³/4 in) that extends beyond the blanket will be folded and stitched to the blanket backing.

3 Stitch the front edge of the lace to the blanket, using a blind hem, then fold the top edge over and stitch it to the back of the blanket, stitching through the backing fabric and into the wool but not through the front lace. Remove all the basting threads.

Smocked Dress

MADE BY DEBBIE BALDWIN, CALIFORNIA

This pretty smocking pattern will delight the little girl in your family and can be adapted to suit any commercial dress pattern with a square yoke.

Fits size: 4

Materials

♣ commercial dress pattern
♣ 2.5 m (2³/₄ yd) of fabric
♣ DMC Stranded Cotton: Pink, Green, White
♣ 2 m (2¹/₄ yd) of lace edging
♣ 50 cm (20 in) of entredeux
♣ four 12 mm (¹/₂ in) buttons
♣ 30 cm (12 in) of piping
♣ matching sewing cotton

Method

See the Smocking Pattern on page 44.

Preparation

Place the pattern pieces for the front bodice and the sleeves on the fabric, but only cut them out in a rough square larger all around than the pattern piece. This is to allow for shrinkage due to smocking. Cut out the rest of the fabric pieces for the dress.

Pleating

1 Pleat fifteen rows (including two holding rows) for the yoke design and four rows on each sleeve. Tie off the yoke pleating threads to approximately 25.5 cm (10 in).

2 Using a narrow zigzag stitch, roll and whip the lace edging to the sleeve edges. Pull up the sleeve pleating threads to approximately 12.7 cm (5 in) and tie them off to prepare for smocking.

Smocking

1 For Row 1, beginning at the centre two pleats and starting with a bottom cable, work to the end of the row. Turn the work and, beginning at the centre, work to the end of the row.

2 For Row 2, mirror-image Row 1.

3 After Rows 1 and 2 are smocked, beginning at the centre front, directly under a bottom cable, stitch a top cable, then with a one-step wave stitch, travel to Row 2 and stitch a bottom cable. Continue across to the side. Turn the work and, beginning at the centre front, stitch to the side.

4 For Rows 3 to 5, beginning on Row 3 at two pleats to the left of the centre front, start with a top cable and stitch five cable stitches. Travel down to Row 4 with a four-step wave. On Row 4, stitch five cables, beginning with a bottom cable. Work a four-step wave up to Row 3 and five cable stitches, beginning with a top cable as before. Continue across the row. Turn the work and complete the other side. Row 4/5 is a mirror image of this.

5 For Rows 5¹/₂ to 8¹/₂, beginning at the centre front on Row 6, begin with a bottom cable and stitch a half-space one-step wave stitch up to Row 5¹/₂ and continue across to the end. Turn the work and repeat to the end. At Row 7, centre front, begin with a bottom cable and, with a three-step wave, travel up to Row 6. Top cable at Row 6, then with a

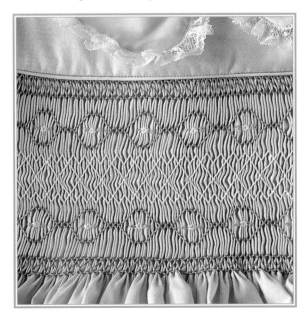

three-step wave, travel back down to Row 7. Repeat across to the end. Turn the work and, beginning again at the centre, stitch to the end. Rows 7 to 8½ are mirror-image rows.

6 Rows 9 to 11 are mirror images of Rows 3 to 5.

7 Rows 12 to 13 are mirror images of Rows 1 to 2.

8 Smock cable rosettes with lazy daisy leaves into the centre of each medallion.

Sleeves

Stitch the cable-wave design as indicated for Rows 1 and 2.

Finishing

Make up the dress and the collar, following the pattern instructions.

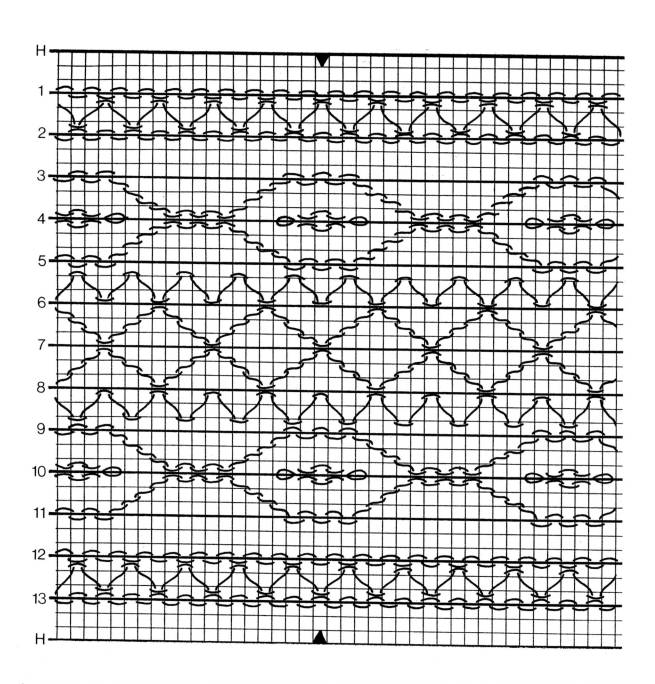

Strawberries

MADE BY PHYLLIS HOFFMAN, McCALLS NEEDLEWORK, USA

This pretty cross stitch design suits beginners and the more experienced alike, and will introduce many stitchers to queen stitch.

Finished size: 7.3 cm x 10.5 cm ($2^7/_8$ in x $4^1/_8$ in)

Stitch count: 68 H x 46 W

Materials

- ❧ 32-count Belfast linen, light mocha
- ❧ DMC Stranded Cotton, one skein each: Salmon 3328, Coral 353, Peach 948, White, Green 3052, Light Green 524, Dark Green 934, Light Gold 738, Medium Gold 436
- ❧ tapestry needle, size 26

Method

See the Cross Stitch Chart on page 48.

1 Following the chart and the colour key, cross stitch over two threads, using two strands of cotton.

2 Backstitch as indicated, using two strands of Salmon. Work the queen stitches (Fig.1), using one strand of cotton.

3 Backstitch the year in two strands of Dark Green.

Queen stitch
Follow figure 1, using one strand of cotton and working over four threads. Bring the needle from the back at 1 and take it to the back of the work at 2. Bring the needle to the front at 3 and take it down at 4, couching the first stitch. Continue stitching in the order indicated.

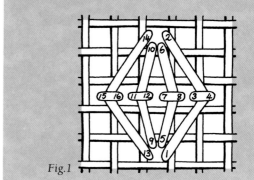

Fig.1

🜲🜲🜲	Dark Green
V V V	Green
\ \ \	Light Green
⬦	Queen Stitch
• •	Peach
⁄ ⁄	Coral
✕ ✕	White
S S S	Medium Gold
◢◢◢	Light Gold
● ● ●	Salmon